the joy of desserts

table of contents

*DF, dairy-free recipe

notes on sweeteners

I use a blend of xylitol, erythritol, and stevia in my recipes. This is twice as sweet as sugar.

It is comparable to Trim Healthy Mama Gentle Sweet and Truvia.

joy filled eats sweetener blend

(twice as sweet as sugar):

INGREDIENTS:

- 1 1/2 cups plus 2 tablespoons erythritol
- 2 cups plus 2 tablespoons xylitol
- 2 tsp pure stevia

INSTRUCTIONS:

Process in the food processor for a few minutes if you are planning on using it in chocolates, beverages, or icing. For baking, you can just mix it together by hand.

alternative sweeteners:

- To sub in Swerve, use 1.5 to 2 times the amount of sweetener called for.

- To sub in Pyure or Trim Healthy Mama Super Sweet, use half the amount of sweetener called for.

Substitutions will work in most recipes. I do not recommend making subs in caramels and candies.

I get a lot of comments from my low carb readers on the use of molasses. I use it for flavor, not sweetness. One teaspoon of molasses has 5 grams of carbs.

Chapter One

cheesecakes, cakes & cupcakes

classic yellow keto birthday cake with chocolate icing

 40 MINS

20 MINS

1 HR

This Classic Yellow Keto Birthday Cake with Chocolate Icing looks just like my mom used to make, thanks to Pillsbury or Betty Crocker. My version is much healthier. It is sugar-free, gluten-free, grain-free, low carb, keto, and a THM S.

ingredients

YELLOW CAKE INGREDIENTS:

- 1 stick of butter softened
- 1/2 cup sugar free sweetener
- 6 eggs
- 2 tsp vanilla
- 1/2 cup whole milk yogurt
- 2 cups almond flour
- 1/2 cup coconut flour
- 2 tsp baking powder
- 1/2 tsp. salt

CHOCOLATE ICING INGREDIENTS:

- 1 stick of butter softened
- 1 cup sugar free sweetener
- 1/2 cup cocoa powder sifted
- 4 tbsp half and half
- 2 tbsp whole milk yogurt
- Sugar free chocolate chips to garnish, if desired

directions

Preheat oven to 350.

In a bowl with an electric mixer cream the butter and sweetener until light and fluffy. Add the yogurt and vanilla and beat until combined. Add the eggs one at a time mixing after each. Stir in the flours, baking powder, and salt until thoroughly combined. Divide batter between 4 round cake pans lined with parchment paper and cooking spray.

Bake at 350 for 20-22 minutes until the cake springs back when lightly pressed with your finger and the edges are golden. Cool completely.

Icing Instructions: Beat the butter and sweetener until smooth. Add the cocoa powder and half and half. Beat until smooth. Add the yogurt. Use to ice the cooled cake.

nutrition facts

Amount Per Serving: 1

Servings: 12 servings

Calories 185

Calories from Fat 117

Total Fat 13g (20%)

Saturated Fat 3g (15%)

Cholesterol 85mg (28%)

Sodium 132mg (6%)

Potassium 196mg (6%)

Total Carbohydrates 10g (3%)

Sugars 1g

Dietary Fiber 4g (16%)

Protein 8g (16%)

Vitamin A (2.9%)

Calcium (11.4%)

Iron (9.9%)

sour cream vanilla cupcakes

 10 MINS

30 MINS

40 MINS

Looking for basic yellow healthy cupcakes? These Sour Cream Vanilla Keto Cupcakes have only 2 net carbs each. They are great plain or with your favorite icing. I also love them with strawberries and whipped cream.

ingredients

- 4 tbsp butter softened
- 1/2 cup sugar free sweetener
- 4 eggs
- 1 tsp vanilla
- 1/4 cup sour cream
- 1 cup almond flour
- 1/4 cup coconut flour
- 1 tsp baking powder
- 1/4 tsp salt

directions

In a bowl with an electric mixer cream the butter and sweetener until light and fluffy. Add the sour cream and vanilla and beat until combined. Add the eggs one at a time mixing after each.

Stir in the flours, baking powder, and salt until thoroughly combined. Divide batter between 12 muffin cups lined with paper liners.

Bake at 350 for 20-25 min. Some ovens will take up to 30. You want the cupcakes to be firm to the touch and golden brown.

nutrition facts

Amount Per Serving: 1

Servings: 12

Calories 128

Calories from Fat 99

Total Fat 11g (17%)

Saturated Fat 4g (20%)

Cholesterol 67mg (22%)

Sodium 112mg (5%)

Potassium 69mg (2%)

Total Carbohydrate 3g (1%)

Dietary Fiber 1g (4%)

Protein 4g (8%)

Vitamin A (4.5%)

Calcium (5.2%)

Iron (3.9%)

black bottom cupcakes

 15 MINS

22 MINS

37 MINS

This is such a classic recipe that I had to come up with a healthier version. Chocolate cake plus cheesecake plus chocolate chunks. Need I say more? Black Bottom Cupcakes are a coffee treat you can enjoy once again.

ingredients

CHOCOLATE CAKE INGREDIENTS:

- 1/2 cup pumpkin puree
- 2 eggs
- 2 tbsp butter softened
- 1/4 cup almond flour
- 1 tbsp coconut flour
- 1/3 cup sugar free sweetener
- 1/3 cup raw cacao or cocoa powder
- 1 tsp vanilla
- 1 tsp baking powder
- pinch salt

CHEESECAKE TOPPING:

- 4 oz cream cheese softened
- 1 egg
- 1/2 tsp vanilla
- 1 tsp butter softened
- 2 tbsp sugar free sweetener
- 2 oz 85% dark chocolate (chopped) or sugar free chocolate chips

directions

Preheat oven to 350.

You can just dump all the chocolate cake ingredients into the bowl at once and mix with an electric mixer. It will end up like a thick chocolate batter. Divide the batter into 12 paper lined muffin tins. Use a spoon to make a well in the center. That is where the cheesecake will go.

In a new bowl (or after you wash the first one) mix 4 oz cream cheese, 1 egg, 1/2 tsp vanilla, 1 tsp butter, and 2 T sweetener. Blend until smooth. Divide the cheesecake batter between the cupcakes.

Sprinkle the tops of the cupcake with the chopped chocolate. Bake at 350 for 22-25 minutes until the cheesecake is slightly firm, puffed up, and turning golden brown around the edges.

Cool for at least 15 minutes before serving. Store in the refrigerator.

nutrition facts

Servings: 12 cupcakes

Calories 96

Calories from Fat 72

Total Fat 8g (12%)

Saturated Fat 3g (15%)

Cholesterol 57mg (19%)

Sodium 67mg (3%)

Potassium 127mg (4%)

Total Carbohydrate 3g (1%)

Dietary Fiber 1g (4%)

Protein 3g (6%)

Vitamin A (36.9%)

Vitamin C (0.5%)

Calcium (4.6%)

Iron (4.7%)

vanilla ricotta cheesecake

15 MINS

1 HR 32 MINS

1 HR 15 MINS

This Vanilla Ricotta Cheesecake Recipe is rich and creamy. If you've never tried ricotta in a cheesecake it works really well. It makes a lighter cheesecake than just using cream cheese. With just 8 simple ingredients I'm sure this will be your new favorite keto cheesecake!

ingredients

CRUST INGREDIENTS:

- 2/3 cup almond flour
- 1/3 cup coconut flour
- 4 tbsp melted butter
- 2 tbsp sugar free sweetener

FILLING INGREDIENTS:

- 2 cups ricotta cheese
- 16 oz cream cheese softened
- 4 eggs
- 1 tbsp vanilla
- 3/4 cup sugar free sweetener

directions

Preheat oven to 350. Wrap a springform pan with three layers of aluminum foil. You are going to bake this in a water bath so this protects the crust from getting wet.

Mix crust ingredients until crumbly. Press into the bottom of the springform pan. Bake for 12 minutes until golden brown around the edges.

Meanwhile, in a food processor or with an electric mixer mix the ricotta cheese until smooth. Add the cream cheese and mix again until combined. Add the eggs, vanilla, and sweetener. Process until smooth. You will probably need to scrape down the sides of the bowl a few times.

When the crust is done grease the sides of the pan with a pat of butter on a fork. Don't touch it to the crust. This will help the cheesecake release from the pan easier. Pour the cheese mixture on top of the crust.

Put the entire pan into a larger pan. Pour hot water into the larger, outside pan. Bake at 350 for 1 hour 10 minutes or until only the very center of the cheesecake jiggles.

Leave the cheesecake in the oven with the oven off for at least one hour. Preferable two hours. Refrigerate for at least 4 hours before serving. To serve run a knife around the edges of the pan and then release the spring mechanism to remove the outside of the pan.

nutrition facts

Amount Per Serving: 1 slice
Servings: 12
Calories 307
Calories from Fat 243
Total Fat 27g (42%)
Saturated Fat 14g (70%)
Cholesterol 127mg (42%)
Sodium 217mg (9%)
Potassium 115mg (3%)
Total Carbohydrates 6g (2%)
Dietary Fiber 1g (4%)
Sugars 1g
Protein 10g (20%)
Vitamin A (17.8%)
Calcium (14.4%)
Iron (4.9%)

no bake cookie dough cheesecake

30 MINS

30 MINS

With a layer of raw chocolate chip cookie dough, a layer of creamy cheesecake, and a layer of rich chocolate ganache my No Bake Cookie Dough Cheesecake may be the best dessert ever.

ingredients

COOKIE DOUGH
INGREDIENTS:

- 2 cups almond flour
- 8 tbsp butter softened
- 2 oz cream cheese softened
- 1/2 cup sugar free sweetener
- 1 tsp molasses
- 2 tsp vanilla
- 2 tsp coconut flour
- 1/2 cup sugar-free chocolate chips

CHEESECAKE
INGREDIENTS:

- 8 oz cream cheese
- 1 cup cottage cheese
- 1/2 cup sugar free sweetener
- 1/4 cup sour cream
- 1/2 tsp vanilla
- 2 tbsp gelatin

GANACHE INGREDIENTS:

- 4 oz unsweetened baking chocolate
- 4 oz heavy cream
- 6 tbsp sugar free sweetener

directions

To make the cookie dough stir together all the
ingredients (except the chocolate chips) until
smooth. Stir in the chocolate chips. Press into the
bottom of a 9-inch springform pan.

For the cheesecake layer, process the cream cheese
and cottage cheese in a food processor until smooth.
Add the sour cream, sweetener, and vanilla. Process
until well combined. While the machine is running
slowly sprinkle in the gelatin. Spread the cheesecake
mixture on top of the cookie dough.

To make the ganache heat the cream until bubbly
in the microwave or a small saucepan. Pour over the
chopped chocolate. Stir until the chocolate melts.
Add the sweetener and stir until smooth. Transfer
to a small blender or food processor. Process for a
minute or two until thick and shiny. This step really
ensures a smooth ganache topping. Pour onto the
cheesecake and spread gently.

Refrigerate for at least 4-6 hours. Carefully run
a knife around the edge before releasing the
springform pan. When serving you have to slide the
pie cutter between the pan and cookie dough before
lifting the slice. Since it is raw dough it is softer than
a traditional graham cracker crust.

nutrition facts

Amount Per Serving: 1

Servings: 16

Calories 299

Calories from Fat 252

Total Fat 28g (43%)

Saturated Fat 13g (65%)

Cholesterol 48mg (16%)

Sodium 166mg (7%)

Potassium 147mg (4%)

Total Carbohydrate 8g (3%)

Dietary Fiber 3g (12%)

Sugars 2g

Protein 8g (16%)

Vitamin A (11.2%)

Calcium (8%)

Iron (14.4%)

Chapter Two

cookies

butter pecan cookies

15 MINS

17 MINS

32 MINS

These Butter Pecan Cookies live up to their name. They are buttery and chock full of pecans. They are crisp, sweet, and are the perfect sweet bite after supper. Whether you need eggless cookies or not these are divine.

ingredients

- 1 stick cold salted butter cut into pieces
- 1 cup almond flour
- 1/3 cup coconut flour
- 2/3 cup sugar free sweetener
- 2 tsp gelatin
- 1 tsp vanilla
- 1 cup pecans

directions

Preheat oven to 350. Line a large cookie sheet with parchment paper.

Combine the butter, almond flour, coconut flour, 1/3 cup of the sweetener, gelatin, and vanilla in a food processor. Pulse until wet crumbs form. Add the pecans. Pulse until they are chopped. The dough will come together into a ball as the pecans are chopped.

Divide the dough into 16 pieces. Put the remaining 1/3 cup sweetener in a shallow bowl. Roll each piece of dough into a ball. Put in the sweetener and press it into a disc. Flip it over and press again so both sides are dusted with sweetener. Put on the prepared baking sheet. Repeat.

Bake for 17-19 minutes or until the edges are golden.

nutrition facts

Amount Per Serving: 1 cookie

Servings: 16 cookies

Calories 146

Calories from Fat 126

Total Fat 14g (22%)

Saturated Fat 4g (20%)

Cholesterol 15mg (5%)

Sodium 56mg (2%)

Potassium 25mg (1%)

Total Carbohydrate 3g (1%)

Dietary Fiber 2g (8%)

Protein 2g (4%)

Vitamin A (3.6%)

Vitamin C (0.1%)

Calcium (2.1%)

Iron (2.7%)

five minute magic cookies

 5 MINS

20 MINS

25 MINS

These Five Minute Magic Cookies take all the flavors of my popular Magic Cookie Bars and turn them into a cookie that mixes up in only 5 minutes. With chocolate chips, coconut flakes, and walnuts these are my new favorite easy recipe.

ingredients

- 2 tbsp coconut cream *
- 2 tbsp butter
- 1/4 cup sugar free sweetener
- 2 egg yolks
- 1/2 cup sugar-free chocolate chips
- 1/2 cup walnuts (or other nuts of your choice)
- 1/2 cup unsweetened flaked coconut

directions

Preheat oven to 350.

Stir together the butter and coconut cream until smooth. Add the sweetener and egg yolks. Mix well. Add the rest of the ingredients. Scoop onto a parchment lined baking sheet to form 12 cookies. Press down to flatten the tops.

Bake for 20 minutes or until golden.

recipe notes

* You can buy small cans of coconut cream or refrigerate a can of full-fat coconut milk until it separates. For this recipe, you need the solid part of the coconut milk.

nutrition facts

Amount Per Serving: 1

Servings: 12

Calories 117

Calories from Fat 99

Total Fat 11g (17%)

Saturated Fat 6g (30%)

Cholesterol 37mg (12%)

Sodium 21mg (1%)

Potassium 97mg (3%)

Total Carbohydrate 3g (1%)

Dietary Fiber 1g (4%)

Protein 2g (4%)

Vitamin A (2%)

Vitamin C (0.1%)

Calcium (1.5%)

Iron (7.5%)

mini carrot cake cookies with cream cheese frosting

 25 MINS

15 MINS

40 MINS

If you are like me and love teeny tiny one bite desserts these will be right up your alley. My Mini Carrot Cake Cookie with Cream Cheese Filling are bursting with flavor in each little cookie.

ingredients

COOKIE INGREDIENTS:

- 2 cups almonds
- 1/4 cup sugar free sweetener
- 2 oz half and half
- 2 tbsp butter
- 2 egg whites
- 1 tsp cinnamon
- 1 tsp baking powder
- 3/4 cup shredded carrots
- 1/2 cup coconut flakes

CREAM CHEESE FILLING:

- 4 oz cream cheese
- 6 tbsp sugar free sweetener
- 2 tbsp butter
- 1 tsp half and half
- 1/2 tsp vanilla

directions

Preheat oven to 350. Line two large cookie sheets with parchment paper.

Process the almonds in a food processor until they start to break down into a nut butter. Stop the machine and scrape the sides down as needed. Add the sweetener, half and half, butter, egg whites, cinnamon, and baking powder. Process until smooth. Stir in the carrots and coconut flakes.

Using a small cookie scoop make about 40 cookies.

Bake for 15 minutes or until firm to the touch and golden around the edges. Cool completely.

Meanwhile, cream together the filling ingredients with an electric mixer until smooth. Put into a piping bag with a small round or star tip. Press the tip halfway down into the center of each cookie. Gently fill with the icing and then swirl on top.

nutrition facts

Amount Per Serving: 1 cookie
Servings: 40 cookies
Calories 71
Calories from Fat 54
Total Fat 6g (9%)
Saturated Fat 2g (10%)
Cholesterol 6mg (2%)
Sodium 22mg (1%)
Potassium 77mg (2%)
Total Carbohydrate 2g (1%)
Dietary Fiber 1g (4%)
Protein 1g (2%)
Vitamin A (1.6%)
Calcium (2.9%)
Iron (1.8%)

almond biscotti cookies

 15 MINS

1 HR

1 HR 15 MINS

My Almond Biscotti Cookies Recipe is a perfect nightcap to a busy day. Sip a cappuccino and indulge in this sweet low carb cookie.

ingredients

- 1 1/2 cups almond flour
- 1/4 cup ground golden flax
- 1/4 cup sugar free sweetener
- 2 tbsp coconut flour
- 2 tsp gelatin
- 1 tsp baking powder
- 1/2 tsp salt
- 1/4 cup coconut oil use refined or butter flavored to avoid a coconutty taste
- 1 egg yolk
- 1 tsp almond extract
- 1/3 cup chopped almonds

OPTIONAL TOPPING:
- 2-3 oz sugar free chocolate melted
- 2 tbsp chopped almonds

directions

Preheat oven to 325.

Combine the almond flour, flax, sweetener, coconut flour, gelatin, baking powder, and salt in a food processor. Pulse to combine. With the machine running slowly pour in the coconut oil, egg yolk, and almond extract. The dough will come together in a ball. Scrape down the sides of the food processor and add the 1/2 cup chopped almonds. Pulse just enough to incorporate the almonds into the batter.

On a parchment-lined baking sheet form the dough into a long rectangular log, about 4 x 10 inches. Bake for 20 minutes.

Remove the dough from the oven and cut the log into 10 pieces. Use a big knife and press down. Wiggle the knife back and forth between the pieces so that there is a gap between them. Return to the oven, reduce the heat to 225 degrees and bake for an additional 40 minutes. Cool completely.

To coat the biscotti in chocolate simply turn on the side and drizzle and spread the chocolate on the bottom. Then flip upright again to coat the top and sides. Sprinkle with the additional chopped almonds.

recipe notes

These are a little too fragile to dip into the melted chocolate. It works better to spread the chocolate on them. They firm up more when chilled.

nutrition facts

Amount Per Serving: 1 cookie
Servings: 12
Calories 197
Calories from Fat 144
Total Fat 16g (25%)
Saturated Fat 5g (25%)
Cholesterol 16mg (5%)
Sodium 236mg (10%)
Potassium 110mg (3%)
Total Carbohydrate 9g (3%)
Dietary Fiber 3g (12%)
Protein 5g (10%)
Vitamin A (0.4%)
Calcium (7.3%)
Iron (5.8%)

peanut butter cup cookies

 15 MINS

15 MINS

30 MINS

My Peanut Butter Cup Cookies are a match made in heaven. With a tender cookie crust, chocolate ganache filling, and the crunch of salty peanuts on top your cravings will be fulfilled.

ingredients

COOKIE INGREDIENTS:

- 2 large eggs room temperature
- 1/2 cup coconut oil melted
- 1/2 cup peanut butter room temperature
- 1 tsp vanilla
- 1/3 cup peanut flour
- 3/4 cup sugar free sweetener
- 1 tsp salt
- 1/2 cup almond flour
- 1/4 cup coconut flour
- 1 tsp aluminum free baking powder

TOPPING INGREDIENTS:

- 3 oz sugar free chocolate chips or chopped chocolate
- 2 oz heavy cream
- 1/4 cup peanuts roasted salted

directions

Preheat oven to 350.

Start by whisking the eggs and melted coconut oil with the peanut butter and vanilla.

Add the peanut butter, powder, sweetener, salt, almond flour, coconut flour and baking powder. Mix until well combined.

Divide the batter between 30 mini muffin cups lined with aluminum liners.

Bake for 14-16 minutes or until golden around the edges. While warm and still in the pan use a tart tamper or the rounded back of a teaspoon to make a well in the center of each cookie. Cool completely.

To make the ganache heat the cream to just before the boiling point. Pour over the chocolate. Stir until it is smooth.

Fill the cooled cookies with the prepared ganache. Top with a few peanuts.

recipe notes

Chill the cookies before removing from the tin if you did not use cupcake liners. After chilling, I set the bottom of the pan in warm water for a few seconds and then ran a small knife around the edges and they popped right out.

nutrition facts

Amount Per Serving: 1

Servings: 30 cookies

Calories 109

Calories from Fat 90

Total Fat 10g (15%)

Saturated Fat 5g (25%)

Cholesterol 13mg (4%)

Sodium 105mg (4%)

Potassium 100mg (3%)

Total Carbohydrate 3g (1%)

Dietary Fiber 1g (4%)

Protein 3g (6%)

Vitamin A (0.9%)

Calcium (2.2%)

Iron (4.7%)

Chapter Three

brownies & bars

little debbie fudge brownies

 10 MINS

20 MINS

30 MINS

My Homemade Little Debbie Fudge Healthy Brownies are better than a copycat version of those favorite lunch box treats. They are rich, fudgy, studded with walnuts and topped with fudge icing.

ingredients

BROWNIE INGREDIENTS:

- 4 oz unsweetened baking chocolate
- 1 1/2 sticks salted butter
- 1 cups sugar free sweetener
- 3 eggs room temperature
- 1/4 cup almond flour
- 2 tbsp coconut flour
- 1 tsp vanilla
- 1/2 tsp salt
- 1 cup walnuts

FUDGE ICING INGREDIENTS:

- 7 oz 85% dark chocolate (I used two 3.5 oz bars)
- 7 oz heavy cream
- 6-8 tbsp sugar free sweetener

directions

Preheat oven to 350. Line a 9 x 13 baking dish with parchment paper or foil and spray with cooking spray.

Melt the unsweetened chocolate and butter in a glass bowl in the microwave. Add the rest of the brownie ingredients and stir until smooth.

Pour into the prepared baking pan and spread evenly. Bake for 20-25 min or until no longer jiggly. Cool completely.

Heat the cream in the microwave for 2 minutes or in a saucepan over medium heat until bubbles form around the edge. Remove from heat and add the chocolate. Stir until melted. Add the sweetener and whisk until smooth and shiny. Pour over the cooled brownies and spread evenly.

Store in the fridge or freeze for later.

nutrition facts

Servings: 24
Calories 193
Calories from Fat 171
Total Fat 19g (29%)
Saturated Fat 10g (50%)
Cholesterol 47mg (16%)
Sodium 114mg (5%)
Potassium 144mg (4%)
Total Carbohydrate 5g (2%)
Dietary Fiber 2g (8%)
Protein 3g (6%)
Vitamin A (6.6%)
Vitamin C (0.1%)
Calcium (3.1%)
Iron (14.2%)

cranberry bliss bars

10 MINS

25 MINS

35 MINS

This delightful keto fall treat is reminiscent of the famous cranberry bliss bars sold at Starbucks with cranberries, hints of orange and ginger, and cream cheese icing.

ingredients

- 6 tbsp softened butter
- 1/3 cup sugar free sweetener
- 1 tsp molasses ***
- pinch salt
- 2 eggs
- 1 tsp vanilla
- 1/2 tsp orange extract
- 1/4 cup almond flour
- 1/4 cup coconut flour
- 1/4 cup ground golden flax (or additional almond flour)
- 1 tsp baking powder

- 1/4 tsp ginger optional
- 1 cup fresh cranberries finely chopped by hand or in a food processor and tossed with 1/2 tsp pure stevia or 2 tbsp of my sweetener

FROSTING:
- 4 oz cream cheese softened
- 1 tbsp butter softened
- 1/2 cup powdered sweetener
- 4 drops lemon extract

recipe notes

*** See notes on molasses on page 7. This recipe makes 16 bars. That is less than .5 grams of carbs from the molasses. If you prefer you can just omit it.

directions

Preheat oven to 350. Grease an 8x8 baking pan.

Cream together butter and sweetener. Add molasses, salt, eggs, and extracts. Mix thoroughly. Add dry ingredients. Mix well. Fold in the cranberries.

Spread in an 8x8 baking dish. Bake for 30-35 min. until golden brown. Allow to cool for 15 minutes.

Meanwhile, mix together the cream cheese, butter, sweetener, and lemon extract until fluffy.

Spread icing very gently on cooled bars. The bars can crumble if you aren't gentle. The best way to do this is to drop little blobs of icing on slightly warm bars and spread using an offset spatula. Top with chopped fresh cranberries mixed with sweetener or dried cranberries.

Refrigerate until cold and cut into squares.

nutrition facts

Amount Per Serving: 1

Servings: 16

Calories 110

Calories from Fat 90

Total Fat 10g (15%)

Saturated Fat 5g (25%)

Cholesterol 41mg (14%)

Sodium 80mg (3%)

Potassium 76mg (2%)

Total Carbohydrate 3g (1%)

Dietary Fiber 1g (4%)

Protein 2g (4%)

Vitamin A (5.6%)

Calcium (3.6%)

Iron (2.4%)

magic cookie bars

 15 MINS

 35 MINS

 50 MINS

If you love this classic treat but want a healthier version you've come to the right place. My Magic Cookie Bars are low carb, keto, grain-free, sugar-free, gluten-free, and Trim Healthy Mama friendly.

ingredients

CRUST:

- 1/4 cup almond flour
- 1/4 cup coconut flour
- 1/4 cup ground golden flax
- 1/4 cup melted butter

SWEETENED CONDENSED MILK:

- 1/4 cup heavy cream
- 2 tbsp butter
- 1/2 cup sugar free sweetener
- 1 egg yolk

TOPPINGS:

- 1/2 cup unsweetened flaked coconut
- 1/2 cup sugar free chocolate chips or chopped 85% dark chocolate
- 1/2 cup chopped walnuts (or other nut of choice)

directions

Combine crust ingredients and press into the bottom of a 8×8 baking dish. Bake at 350 for 12 min. or until golden brown.

Meanwhile, you need to make my sugar free condensed milk. Bring the heavy cream, 2 tablespoons butter, and sweetener to a gentle boil and cook stirring frequently until it is light golden brown and thick enough to coat the back of a spoon.

Remove from the heat. Either cool until room temperature before stirring in the egg yolk OR, if you are impatient like me, very slowly pour the liquid over the egg yolk while whisking like crazy. (No one wants scrambled yolk in their magic cookie bars).

Now it is time to assemble. Sprinkle coconut, chocolate chips, and walnuts onto the crust. Drizzle condensed milk over the top. Bake at 350 for 20-25 min. until set and golden brown. Cool completely and chill in the fridge before serving or the crust can crumble.

nutrition facts

Servings: 16

Calories 148

Calories from Fat 126

Total Fat 14g (22%)

Saturated Fat 7g (35%)

Cholesterol 28mg (9%)

Sodium 46mg (2%)

Potassium 88mg (3%)

Total Carbohydrate 4g (1%)

Dietary Fiber 2g (8%)

Protein 2g (4%)

Vitamin A (4.1%)

Calcium (2.4%)

Iron (6.7%)

tagalong peanut butter cookie bars

 35 MINS

25 MINS

60 MINS

The Girl Scout cookie favorite made into a healthy bar with only 6 ingredients and ready in under an hour. My Tagalong Peanut Butter Cookie Bars will help you resist cookie sale temptation.

ingredients

SHORTBREAD COOKIE LAYER:

- 3/4 cups almond flour
- 3 tbsp sugar free sweetener
- pinch of salt
- 3 tbsp butter softened
- 1 tsp vanilla

PEANUT BUTTER LAYER:

- 1/2 cup peanut butter
- 3 tbsp sugar free sweetener
- 1/2 tsp vanilla

CHOCOLATE LAYER:

- 3.5 oz 85% dark chocolate or sugar free chocolate chopped

directions

Preheat oven to 350.

In a medium bowl mix all the shortbread ingredients until combined. Press into the bottom of a square 8x8 baking dish.

Bake for 15-20 minutes or until golden brown.

Meanwhile, combine the peanut butter ingredients. If your peanut butter is cold you can microwave it for 30 seconds to soften it.

When the shortbread comes out of the oven drop little blobs of the peanut on top of it. Spread gently with a spatula. The heat from the cookie will help spread the peanut butter. Be gentle or the bottom layer can crumble.

Melt the chocolate in the microwave or double boiler. Pour over the peanut butter. Spread gently. Put in the refrigerator until firm. Cut into squares and enjoy!

nutrition facts

Servings: 16 bars

Calories 128

Calories from Fat 108

Total Fat 12g (18%)

Saturated Fat 4g (20%)

Cholesterol 5mg (2%)

Sodium 57mg (2%)

Potassium 103mg (3%)

Total Carbohydrate 4g (1%)

Dietary Fiber 2g (8%)

Sugars 1g

Protein 3g (6%)

Vitamin A (1.3%)

Calcium (2.1%)

Iron (7.9%)

raspberry cheesecake brownies

10 MINS

35 MINS

45 MINS

My Dark Chocolate Raspberry Cheesecake Brownies are the perfect dessert or grab and go snack. With the flavors of chocolate, raspberries, and cheesecake they will be your new favorite treat.

ingredients

BROWNIE INGREDIENTS:

- 1/2 cup melted butter
- 1/2 cup warm water
- 2 large eggs room temperature
- 2/3 cup sugar free sweetener
- 1/2 cup almond flour
- 1/3 cup cocoa powder
- 1/4 cup coconut flour
- 1 tsp vanilla
- 3/4 tsp baking powder
- 3/4 tsp salt

TOPPING INGREDIENTS:

- 3.5 oz bar 85% dark chocolate chopped (or sugar free chocolate of choice)
- 8 oz cream cheese
- 2 tbsp sugar free sweetener
- 1 cup frozen raspberries

directions

Preheat oven to 350. Grease a 9 x 9 baking dish.

In a large bowl whisk together the butter, warm water, and eggs. Add the dry ingredients and mix well. Pour into the baking dish. Sprinkle the chopped chocolate on top of the batter.

In a small bowl stir together the cream cheese and 1 tablespoon sweetener. Drop dollops on top of the batter and swirl gently.

Scatter the frozen raspberries on top. Sprinkle with the additional tablespoon of sweetener.

Bake for 35-40 minutes or until the entire brownie has puffed up and is no longer jiggly in the center.

nutrition facts

Amount Per Serving: 1
Servings: 16 brownies
Calories 174
Calories from Fat 144
Total Fat 16g (25%)
Saturated Fat 9g (45%)
Cholesterol 51mg (17%)
Sodium 219mg (9%)
Potassium 140mg (4%)
Total Carbohydrate 6g (2%)
Dietary Fiber 3g (12%)
Sugars 1g
Protein 3g (6%)
Vitamin A (7.9%)
Vitamin C (2.4%)
Calcium (4.7%)
Iron (9.6%)

Chapter Four

pies & tarts

blackberry custard pie

 10 MINS

55 MINS

1 HR 5 MINS

I love pretty desserts and this Blackberry Custard Pie is as pretty as they come. With a press in pie crust & blender custard it has just 10 minutes of prep time.

ingredients

EASY LOW CARB PIE CRUST INGREDIENTS:
- 1 1/3 cups almond flour
- 1 1/2 tsp coconut flour
- 2 tbsp cold butter
- 1 1/2 tsp cold water

FILLING INGREDIENTS:
- 10 oz frozen blackberries
- 3 eggs
- 4 tbsp butter softened
- 1/2 cup sugar free sweetener
- 1 tbsp vanilla
- 1/4 cup almond flour

directions

Preheat oven to 350.

Put the almond flour, coconut flour, and butter in a food processor and pulse until crumbs form. Add the water and pulse until it comes together in a dough. Press into the bottom and up the sides of a pie plate. Prick the bottom with a fork. Bake for 10 minutes.

Remove from the oven and scatter the blackberries over the crust.

Combine the rest of the ingredients in a blender and blend until smooth. Pour the custard over the berries.

Bake for 40-50 minutes until the center isn't jiggly and the pie is golden brown. Cool completely and then chill in the fridge for a few hours before serving.

recipe notes

Feel free to sub in any berries of your choice. This is delicious with blueberries and raspberries!

nutrition facts

Amount Per Serving: 1 slice
Servings: 8 slices
Calories 249
Calories from Fat 189
Total Fat 21g (32%)
Saturated Fat 6g (30%)
Cholesterol 84mg (28%)
Sodium 101mg (4%)
Potassium 80mg (2%)
Total Carbohydrate 8g (3%)
Dietary Fiber 4g (16%)
Sugars 2g
Protein 7g (14%)
Vitamin A (8.6%)
Vitamin C (9%)
Calcium (6.8%)
Iron (7.6%)

giant chocolate chip cookie tart

5 MINS

30 MINS

35 MINS

My Giant Chocolate Chip Cookie Tart looks like one huge chocolate chip cookie. With only 6 ingredients and a very easy prep, you can have this scrumptious treat in your oven in five minutes.

ingredients

- 3 cups walnut halves or other nut of choice
- 1 stick butter cold and cut into small pieces
- 1/2 cup sugar free sweetener
- 1 tsp gelatin
- 1 tsp vanilla
- 3/4 cup sugar-free chocolate chips

directions

Preheat oven to 350. Line a tart pan with parchment paper.

Pulse nuts in a food processor until they form fine crumbs. Add the butter, sweetener, gelatin, and vanilla. Pulse until smooth. Spread in the prepared tart pan.

Sprinkle the chocolate chips on top of the batter. Press down slightly.

Bake for 30 minutes or until golden. The center will still be a bit jiggly but will firm up as the tart cools. Do not overbake.

recipe notes

This is a fun birthday cake for kids and kids at heart. You can write a message on top with your favorite icing.

nutrition facts

Servings: 8

Calories 353

Calories from Fat 315

Total Fat 35g (54%)

Saturated Fat 6g (30%)

Sodium 5mg (0%)

Potassium 296mg (8%)

Total Carbohydrate 9g (3%)

Dietary Fiber 4g (16%)

Sugars 1g

Protein 8g (16%)

Vitamin A (0.2%)

Vitamin C (0.7%)

Calcium (5.5%)

Iron (19.1%)

easy strawberry tart

 10 MINS

 10 MINS

This is the easiest Strawberry Tart Recipe ever. With only 5 ingredients and about 10 minutes of prep time, you can still impress your friends and family.

ingredients

CRUST:

- 1.5 cups almond flour
- 3 tbsp butter cut into pieces
- 1/4 cup sugar free sweetener

FILLING:

- 16 oz cream cheese
- 1/2 cup sugar free sweetener
- 2-4 cups strawberries *** quartered

directions

Combine the crust ingredients in a food processor and pulse until a smooth dough forms. Press into the bottom of a 9-inch tart pan.

Add the cream cheese and sweetener to the food processor. Pulse until smooth. Spread on top of the crust. Top with the strawberries. Chill for 2-3 hours before serving.

recipe notes

*** If you are counting macros you probably want to only use 2 cups of strawberries on top of this tart. I do not count macros on Trim Healthy Mama so I used about 4 cups on mine.

nutrition facts

Amount Per Serving: 1 slice

Servings: 8

Calories 362

Calories from Fat 306

Total Fat 34g (52%)

Saturated Fat 14g (70%)

Cholesterol 73mg (24%)

Sodium 220mg (9%)

Potassium 133mg (4%)

Total Carbohydrate 9g (3%)

Dietary Fiber 2g (8%)

Sugars 4g

Protein 8g (16%)

Vitamin A (17.9%)

Vitamin C (25.7%)

Calcium (10.7%)

Iron (6.4%)

lemon ricotta pie

15 MINS

15 MINS

30 MINS

Lemon Ricotta Pie is a favorite in my house. It is light and refreshing and takes less than 15 minutes hands-on time. It is similar to a cheesecake but more refreshing on a hot summer day.

ingredients

- 1 recipe Easy Low Carb Pie Crust (on page 46) or your favorite crust

FILLING INGREDIENTS:

- 2 cups whole milk ricotta cheese
- 4 oz cream cheese softened
- 1/2 cup sugar free sweetener
- 1 tsp fresh lemon juice
- 1/2 tsp finely grated lemon zest
- 2 tsp gelatin

OPTIONAL TOPPING:

- 1 cup fresh blueberries washed and dried, or other berries of your choice

directions

Prepare pie crust as directed and bake until golden brown, about 15 minutes. Let cool.

Combine the first five ingredients for the filling in a food processor and blend until smooth. With the machine running slowly pour in the gelatin. Blend until smooth.

Spread on top of the cooled pie crust. Refrigerate for at least 3-4 hours.

Top with berries or whipped cream, if desired. Serve. Store any leftovers in the fridge.

recipe notes

The nutrition is calculated using one cup of blueberries. Feel free to use more blueberries to cover the top or other berries of your choice.

nutrition facts

Amount Per Serving: 1
Servings: 10
Calories 243
Calories from Fat 180
Total Fat 20g (31%)
Saturated Fat 8g (40%)
Cholesterol 37mg (12%)
Sodium 79mg (3%)
Potassium 78mg (2%)
Total Carbohydrate 7g (2%)
Dietary Fiber 2g (8%)
Sugars 2g
Protein 10g (20%)
Vitamin A (7.6%)
Vitamin C (2.1%)
Calcium (11.3%)
Iron (1.5%)

samoas coconut pie

 20 MINS

60 MINS

1 HR 20 MINS

This Chocolate Caramel Samoas Coconut Pie Recipe is somewhere between a coconut custard pie and a Samoa cookie. With layers of chocolate, caramel, and a cookie crust it will be your new favorite dessert.

ingredients

CARAMEL INGREDIENTS:

- 13.5 oz coconut milk
- 1/3 cup sugar free sweetener
- 1 tbsp butter flavored coconut oil
- 1/2 tsp molasses
- 1 tsp caramel extract

CRUST INGREDIENTS:

- 1/4 cup coconut oil
- 1 cup almond flour
- 3 tbsp coconut flour
- 1.5 tbsp sugar free sweetener
- 1 tsp gelatin
- 1/2 tsp vanilla
- 1/3 cup sugar-free chocolate chips

FILLING INGREDIENTS:

- 13.5 oz coconut milk
- 8 oz unsweetened coconut flakes about 1 3/4 cups
- 2 eggs
- 2 tbsp sugar free sweetener
- 1 tbsp coconut flour

TOPPING:

- 1/2 cup sugar-free chocolate chips melted

directions

Preheat oven to 350.

First, you are going to get the caramel going. Combine the coconut milk, sweetener, butter flavored coconut oil, and molasses in a small saucepan and simmer over medium-low heat, stirring occasionally, until thickened and browned. About 1 hour. Stir in the caramel extract.

Meanwhile, combine almond and coconut flour, coconut oil, 3 tbsp sweetener, gelatin, and vanilla in a food processor and pulse until crumbs form. Press into the bottom of a deep dish pie plate. Bake for 15 minutes. Remove from the oven and sprinkle the 1/3 cup chocolate chips on top. Let sit for 3-4 minutes until they have melted. Gently spread with a spatula. Some crumbs from the crust will get mixed in but keep gently spreading until the chocolate covers the crust.

Combine the filling ingredients in a large mixing bowl. Spread on top of the chocolate covered crust. Bake for 35 minutes. Broil for 2-3 minutes, watching continuously, to toast the coconut on top.

Poke little holes in the top of the pie (use a skewer, not a straw, or you will be able to see them after chilling - lesson learned). Drizzle the caramel over the baked pie. Drizzle with melted chocolate. Chill for at least 2-3 hours. I prefer this cold.

nutrition facts

Amount Per Serving: 1

Servings: 12

Calories 420

Calories from Fat 369

Total Fat 41g (63%)

Saturated Fat 31g (155%)

Cholesterol 27mg (9%)

Sodium 33mg (1%)

Potassium 333mg (10%)

Total Carbohydrate 12g (4%)

Dietary Fiber 6g (24%)

Sugars 2g

Protein 7g (14%)

Vitamin A (0.8%)

Vitamin C (1.1%)

Calcium (4.9%)

Iron (27%)

Chapter Five

candies

pecan pralines

5 MINS

10 MINS

15 MINS

These Pecan Pralines are creamy and sweet with toasted pecans throughout. My Pecan Pralines Recipe cooks in about ten minutes and is ready to eat in under an hour.

ingredients

- 1 cup pecans toasted
- 5 tbsp unsalted butter divided
- 6 tbsp heavy cream
- 1/3 cup sugar free sweetener
- 1/4 tsp vanilla
- Pinch of salt

directions

Combine 4 tbsp of the butter with the sweetener and cream over medium heat. Stir until sweetener is dissolved.

Add the vanilla.

Cook until it is a deep golden brown. As soon as it reaches that deep color (right before burning) remove from the heat and immediately add the other 1 tbsp butter. Stir until smooth.

Add the salt and toasted pecans. Drop by spoonfuls onto on wax paper. Refrigerate until firm.

recipe notes

I toast nuts at 400 degrees until they are lightly browned and smell heavenly.

nutrition facts

Amount Per Serving: 1

Servings: 10 pralines

Calories 145

Calories from Fat 135

Total Fat 15g (23%)

Saturated Fat 5g (25%)

Cholesterol 25mg (8%)

Sodium 3mg (0%)

Potassium 49mg (1%)

Total Carbohydrate 1g (0%)

Protein 1g (2%)

Vitamin A (5.5%)

Vitamin C (0.1%)

Calcium (1.5%)

Iron (1.4%)

peanut butter balls

 20 MINS

 20 MINS

Healthy Peanut Butter Balls with just 4 ingredients! Yes, I did! These are perfect for your chocolate peanut butter craving!

ingredients

- 1 cup salted peanuts finely chopped (not peanut flour)
- 1 cup peanut butter
- 1 cup powdered erythritol such as swerve
- 8 oz sugar-free chocolate chips

directions

Mix together the chopped peanuts, peanut butter, and sweetener. Divide the dough into 18 pieces and shape into balls. Place on a wax paper lined baking sheet. Refrigerate until cold.

Melt the chocolate chips in the microwave or on top of a double boiler. I microwave chocolate chips, stirring every 30 seconds until they are 75% melted. Then I just stir until the rest melt.

Dip each peanut butter ball in the chocolate and place back on the wax paper. Refrigerate until the chocolate sets.

nutrition facts

Amount Per Serving: 1 peanut butter ball

Servings: 18

Calories 194

Calories from Fat 153

Total Fat 17g (26%)

Saturated Fat 6g (30%)

Sodium 103mg (4%)

Potassium 260mg (7%)

Total Carbohydrate 7g (2%)

Dietary Fiber 3g (12%)

Sugars 1g

Protein 7g (14%)

Calcium (2.7%)

Iron (14.7%)

salted caramel cups

15 MINS

10 MINS

25 MINS

Salted Caramel is one of my favorite flavor combinations. I love anything with salted caramel. Especially chocolate. I was inspired to fill dark chocolate with salted caramel and I'm glad I did. These caramel cups are divine.

ingredients

- 4 oz butter
- 8 oz heavy cream
- 1/2 cup + 2 tbsp sugar free sweetener
- 1.5 oz cream cheese
- 1 tsp vanilla extract
- 1 tsp caramel extract
- 1 tsp fine sea salt
- course sea salt for sprinkling on top
- 3.5 - 6 oz 85% dark chocolate or sugar free chocolate ***

directions

Combine the butter, cream, and sweetener in a small saucepan over medium-low heat. Cook until light brown and thickened stirring frequently. This takes 10-15 min.

Stir in the extracts, cream cheese, and salt. Stir until the cream cheese is thoroughly incorporated. Set aside to cool to room temperature and thicken further.

Melt the chocolate in the microwave or in a double boiler. I do it in the microwave stirring every 30 seconds. Put a little in the bottom of each mold and spread it up the sides. Put in the fridge to harden. Do one more layer of chocolate. Harden in the fridge.

Fill the chocolate cups 3/4 full with the room temperature caramel. Put in the fridge to chill the caramel. After about 5 min it should be cool enough to put chocolate on top. You can cover the caramel or just drizzle lines on. Sprinkle with a little coarse sea salt. Store in the fridge.

recipe notes

*** If you cover the tops with chocolate you will need the full amount, if you drizzle lines on top then the lesser amount will work.

nutrition facts

Amount Per Serving: 1 candy

Servings: 30 candies

Calories 77

Calories from Fat 72

Total Fat 8g (12%)

Saturated Fat 5g (25%)

Cholesterol 20mg (7%)

Sodium 112mg (5%)

Potassium 38mg (1%)

Total Carbohydrate 1g (0%)

Vitamin A (4.5%)

Vitamin C (0.1%)

Calcium (1.1%)

Iron (3.7%)

chewy almond joy candies

 20 MINS

 20 MINS

You won't miss this candy bar favorite any longer. With my healthy version of the classic Almond Joy candies, you can indulge without guilt.

ingredients

- 1/3 cup sugar free sweetener
- 1 tsp vanilla
- 1 cup finely shredded coconut
- 2 tbsp coconut oil
- 3 tbsp canned coconut milk
- Pinch of salt
- 3.5 oz 85% dark chocolate or sugar free chocolate
- 24 whole almonds or more if you make smaller bars

directions

Melt coconut oil and coconut milk (if its solid) in the microwave. It takes about 30 seconds. Stir in the sweetener, coconut, vanilla, and salt.

Shape into 12 bars and press almonds into the tops.

Melt the chocolate. I do this by breaking the chocolate bar into chunks and microwaving on high for 30 seconds. Stir. Microwave 30 more seconds. Stir. Repeat. Once it is 80% melted stop microwaving and just stir until it completely melted.

Drizzle chocolate on the top and sides of the bars. I used an offset spatula to get the bottom part of the sides. Refrigerate or freeze until the chocolate is hard.

Flip bars over and coat the bottoms. They look prettier if you can manage to cover all the coconut but they are delicious either way. If you want them to look professional do two coats of chocolate and move them to new wax paper before refrigerating.

nutrition facts

Amount Per Serving: 1 candy

Servings: 12

Calories 128

Calories from Fat 117

Total Fat 13g (20%)

Saturated Fat 9g (45%)

Sodium 5mg (0%)

Potassium 131mg (4%)

Total Carbohydrate 4g (1%)

Dietary Fiber 2g (8%)

Protein 2g (4%)

Vitamin C (0.3%)

Calcium (1.5%)

Iron (10.1%)

buttery walnut toffee

10 MINS

20 MINS

30 MINS

Buttery Walnut Toffee Candy. Homemade toffee is so easy but so satisfying. It looks and tastes like the expensive toffee bark in fancy chocolate shops.

ingredients

- 5 tbsp butter
- 1 cup chopped walnuts
- 5 tbsp heavy cream
- 1/2 cup sugar free sweetener
- pinch of salt
- 7 oz sugar free or very dark chocolate***

directions

Line a small baking pan with foil and spray with cooking spray.

Melt butter over low medium heat until it starts to turn golden. Add nuts and cook for about five minutes until they are slightly toasted. Add 4 tbsp of the cream and the sweetener. Cook until thickened and golden. This takes about 10 minutes. If it doesn't seem to be thickening you can turn up the heat to medium or medium high but stir constantly. It can burn quickly. Remove immediately from the heat and add the salt and reserved cream. Stir until smooth. Pour onto the foil lined tray and refrigerate until firm to the touch (about half an hour).

Melt the chocolate. I do this in a glass bowl in the microwave stirring every thirty seconds. Add sweetener if needed. Pour half of the chocolate on top of the toffee. Put in the freezer until the chocolate is solid. Flip over the toffee bark and peel off the foil. Put the foil back on the tray and put the toffee on chocolate side down. Pour the rest of the chocolate on top. Refrigerate or freeze until firm.

The filling stays soft like a caramel for the first few hours but hardens like a toffee overnight.

recipe notes

***I used two 3.5 oz 90% bars and added 1/3 cup
sweetener- make sure to use chocolate that you like
- you can really taste it in this recipe - if you use
very dark or unsweetened chocolate just sweeten it
to taste.

nutrition facts

Amount Per Serving: 1

Servings: 24

Calories 105

Calories from Fat 99

Total Fat 11g (17%)

Saturated Fat 5g (25%)

Cholesterol 10mg (3%)

Sodium 24mg (1%)

Potassium 92mg (3%)

Total Carbohydrate 3g (1%)

Dietary Fiber 1g (4%)

Protein 1g (2%)

Vitamin A (2.4%)

Vitamin C (0.1%)

Calcium (1.6%)

Iron (8.8%)

Chapter Six

ice cream & frozen treats

peanut butter ice cream

20 MINS

10 MINS

30 MINS

Peanut butter ice cream is my husband's favorite. This rich ice cream is even more amazing topped with homemade caramel and roasted salted nuts.

ingredients

- 2 cups heavy cream
- 2 cups almond milk
- 1/2 cup sugar free sweetener
- 1 tbsp vanilla
- 1 tbsp glycerin
- 3 egg yolks
- 1/2 cup peanut flour

PEANUTTY CARAMEL SAUCE:
(makes enough for about 2-3 sundaes - double if desired)

- 4 tbsp butter
- 4 tbsp heavy cream
- 1/2 cup sugar free sweetener
- 1/2 tsp vanilla
- 1/2 tsp salt
- 2 tbsp peanut flour

directions

Ice Cream Directions: Combine all the ingredients in a blender and blend until smooth. Churn in an ice cream maker according to your manufacturer's instructions. For hard ice cream freeze the ice cream until firm. At least 2 hours. For softer ice cream you can eat some right from the machine.

Caramel Sauce Directions: Combine first three ingredients and cook over medium low heat until bubbly, slightly thickened, and lightly browned. Remove from the heat and add the other ingredients. Cool to room temperature. Store in the fridge. If it solidifies just reheat and stir for it to come back together.

The Ultimate Peanut Butter Caramel Sundae: Peanut Butter Ice Cream + Peanutty Caramel Sauce + Roasted Salted Peanuts = Heaven on Earth

recipe notes

If you are concerned about using raw egg yolks you can purchase pasteurized eggs or you can temper the ice cream base.

The glycerin helps the ice cream to stay scoopable in the freezer. If you don't mind letting the ice cream sit out at room temperature for about half an hour before scooping you can omit the glycerin.

nutrition facts

Calories 396
Total Fat 40.1g (62%)
Saturated Fat 26.2g (131%)
Cholesterol 145mg (48%)
Sodium 216mg (9%)
Total Carbohydrate 6.3g (2%)
Dietary Fiber 2.1g (8%)
Sugars 2.7g
Protein 5.6g
Vitamin A (16%)
Vitamin C (3%)
Calcium (5%)
Iron (9%)

vanilla latte coffee ice cream

 45 MINS

 45 MINS

My Vanilla Latte Coffee Ice Cream is a low carb, sugar-free, rich & creamy ice cream with flavors of coffee & vanilla. A perfect dessert when you crave coffee on a hot summer day.

ingredients

- 2 cups heavy cream
- 1 cup strong coffee
- 1 cup half and half
- 1/2 cup sugar free sweetener
- 1 tbsp vanilla extract
- 2 tbsp instant coffee
- 1 tsp glycerin optional, but recommended – this keeps the ice cream soft enough to scoop
- 3 egg yolks

directions

Combine all ingredients in a blender. Blend until smooth. Pour into an ice cream machine. Freeze according to the manufacturer's instructions.

recipe notes

If you are concerned about using raw egg yolks you can purchase pasteurized eggs or you can temper the ice cream base.

The glycerin helps the ice cream to stay scoopable in the freezer. If you don't mind letting the ice cream sit out at room temperature for about half an hour before scooping you can omit the glycerin.

nutrition facts

Servings: 8

Calories 279

Calories from Fat 243

Total Fat 27g (42%)

Saturated Fat 16g (80%)

Cholesterol 165mg (55%)

Sodium 40mg (2%)

Potassium 150mg (4%)

Total Carbohydrate 5g (2%)

Sugars 1g

Protein 3g (6%)

Vitamin A (21.6%)

Vitamin C (0.8%)

Calcium (8.1%)

Iron (1.3%)

dairy free chocolate ice cream

 5 MINS

5 MINS

This Chocolate Dairy Free Ice Cream Recipe will tempt your taste buds before you even get it into the freezer. With just five minutes of prep, you can have homemade ice cream in no time.

ingredients

- 2 cans coconut milk
- 3/4 cups almond milk
- 3/4 cups cocoa
- 2/3 cups sugar free sweetener
- 3 egg yolks
- 2 tsp glycerin
- 1 tsp vanilla
- 1/2 tsp instant coffee

directions

Put all the ingredients in a blender. Blend until smooth. Pour into an ice cream machine and freeze according to the manufacturer's instructions.

recipe notes

If you are concerned about using raw egg yolks you can purchase pasteurized eggs or you can temper the ice cream base.

The glycerin helps the ice cream to stay scoopable in the freezer. If you don't mind letting the ice cream sit out at room temperature for about half an hour before scooping you can omit the glycerin.

nutrition facts

Servings: 12
Calories 188
Calories from Fat 162
Total Fat 18g (28%)
Saturated Fat 14g (70%)
Cholesterol 48mg (16%)
Sodium 34mg (1%)
Potassium 262mg (7%)
Total Carbohydrate 8g (3%)
Dietary Fiber 3g (12%)
Sugars 3g
Protein 3g (6%)
Vitamin A (1.3%)
Vitamin C (2.3%)
Calcium (4.2%)
Iron (10.9%)

chocolate chip cookie dough ice cream sandwiches

 30 MINS

 30 MINS

If you don't have an ice cream machine you can use store bought low carb ice cream in between the layers of cookie dough.

ingredients

COOKIE DOUGH INGREDIENTS:

- 4 tbsp butter
- 4 tbsp cream cheese
- 2 cups almond flour
- 1/2 cup sugar free sweetener
- 1 tsp molasses
- 1 tsp vanilla
- 1 cup sugar free chocolate chips or chopped sugar free or dark chocolate

ICE CREAM INGREDIENTS:

- 2 cups heavy cream
- 1 cup half and half
- 1 cup almond milk
- 3 egg yolks
- 1/2 cup sugar free sweetener
- 1 tbsp vanilla
- 1 tbsp glycerin
- 1 cup sugar free chocolate chips optional

directions

Line a 8x8 square baking pan with parchment paper or foil.

Beat butter, cream cheese, and sweetener with an electric mixer. Add in the almond flour, sweetener, vanilla, and molasses. Mix well. Stir in the chocolate chips. Put half the cookie dough in the bottom of the pan and spread gently. Cover with another layer of parchment or foil. Spread the rest of the dough onto the second layer. Put this in the freezer.

Meanwhile, make the ice cream. Combine all the ice cream ingredients in a blender. Blend until smooth. Pour into an ice cream machine and churn according to the manufacturers instructions. Add the additional chocolate chips during the last minute if desired. When the ice cream has gotten firm remove the cookie dough from the freezer and take out the top layer. Pour 3/4 of the ice cream on top of the bottom layer of cookie dough. Save the rest in another container.

It is best to not top it with the top cookie dough yet. You need it to firm up a little more. So put this and the top layer of dough in the freezer separately. After an hour or two remove them from the freezer and top the ice cream with the top layer of cookie dough.

Freeze for an additional 3-4 hours. This is when it's nice that there was bit of ice cream left over. It's so hard to be that patient. Eat a little of the extra while you wait.

Remove from the freezer and cut into squares with a sharp knife. Wrap individually with plastic wrap to store.

nutrition facts

Servings: 16
Calories 301
Calories from Fat 261
Total Fat 29g (45%)
Saturated Fat 13g (65%)
Cholesterol 94mg (31%)
Sodium 79mg (3%)
Total Carbohydrate 8g (3%)
Dietary Fiber 2g (8%)
Sugars 2g
Protein 5g (10%)
Vitamin A (13.5%)
Vitamin C (0.4%)
Calcium (10.1%)
Iron (11.6%)

frozen hot chocolate

 5 MINS
 5 MINS

Frozen Hot Chocolate. It doesn't make much sense until you taste it. Then you realize how it is possible to capture the flavor of a hot chocolate in a frozen beverage.

ingredients

- 3 tbsp heavy cream
- 1 cup almond milk
- 3 tbsp sugar free sweetener
- 3 tbsp dark cocoa powder
- 1/2 tsp vanilla
- pinch of xanthan gum optional (helps stop the drink from separating)
- 1 tbsp coconut oil
- 14 ice cubes

directions

Combine all the ingredients and blend until smooth.

nutrition facts

Servings: 1
Calories 350
Calories from Fat 315
Total Fat 35g (54%)
Saturated Fat 23g (115%)
Cholesterol 61mg (20%)
Sodium 355mg (15%)
Potassium 246mg (7%)
Total Carbohydrate 11g (4%)
Dietary Fiber 6g (24%)
Protein 5g (10%)
Vitamin A (13.2%)
Calcium (35%)
Iron (12.5%)

Made in the USA
Lexington, KY
27 April 2019